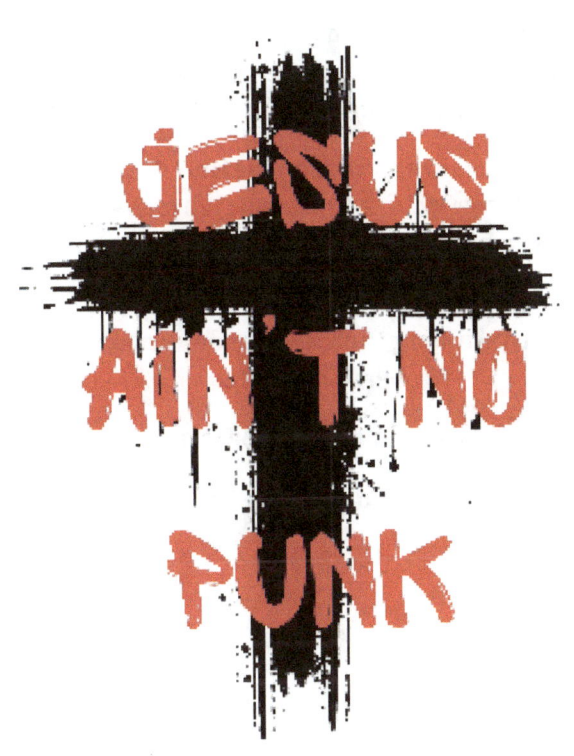

PUBLISHED IN THE UNITED STATES OF AMERICA
FIRST PRINTING, 2025

COVER DESIGN BY KELLY BRADLEY

PRINTED BY AMAZON KDP

TABLE OF CONTENTS

Introduction:

Jesus Ain't No Punk

Let's be real: often when we see Jesus portrayed in art and media, we see this dude looking docile with his arms stretched open and a slight head tilt and you just hear the soft "ahhhhh" of angels singing in the distance. Jesus gets painted like He was soft. Gentle, quiet, passive, always smiling with kids on His lap and never causing any drama. While it's true that He was full of compassion and grace, those are parts of Him, but that just ain't it. When you really read the Gospels, you see a different side - a Savior who was bold, fearless, unshaken, and unapologetically real. Jesus wasn't shy. He wasn't scared of confrontation. He wasn't worried about people's opinions. Jesus ain't no punk.

This devotional is about getting to know *that* Jesus. The Jesus who faced down Satan in the wilderness and didn't flinch. The Jesus who called out hypocrisy right to the Pharisees' faces. The Jesus who walked straight into places others avoided—whether it was the home of a tax collector, the tomb of a dead man, or the cross itself. The Jesus who flipped tables, silenced storms, cast out demons, healed the broken, defended the rejected, and declared His authority with fire.

But here's the key: this isn't just about admiring Jesus' boldness from a distance. It's about realizing what that means for *us*. If Jesus ain't no punk—and we're His followers—then neither are we.

That means:

- We're called to walk in courage, not fear.

- We're called to stand in truth, even when it costs us.

- We're called to live on mission with urgency, not comfort.

- We're called to love boldly, forgive freely, and worship loudly.

Every section of this devotional will take you into a moment in the Gospels where Jesus showed His strength, His authority, and His unshakable confidence in His Father's plan. Along the way, you'll be challenged to ask yourself real questions: Am I following Jesus fully, or holding back? Am I living bold or living safe? Am I standing on His authority—or letting something else call the shots?

By the end of this journey, my prayer is simple: that you'll see Jesus more clearly, follow Him more fully, and walk in the kind of strength that reflects who He truly is. Most of all, I pray that you are filled with boldness to share these sides of Jesus with others who may need a strong savior more than a seemingly passive one.

Because Jesus ain't no punk—and if you're His, neither are you.

DAY 1

AIN'T NO PUNK IN THE WILDERNESS

Scripture Reading

Matthew 4:1–11 (NLT)

Then Jesus was led by the Spirit into the wilderness to be tempted there by the devil. For forty days and forty nights he fasted and became very hungry. During that time the devil came and said to him, "If you are the Son of God, tell these stones to become loaves of bread."

But Jesus told him, "No! The Scriptures say, 'People do not live by bread alone, but by every word that comes from the mouth of God.'"

Then the devil took him to the holy city, Jerusalem, to the highest point of the Temple, and said, "If you are the Son of God, jump off! For the Scriptures say,
'He will order his angels to protect you.
And they will hold you up with their hands
so you won't even hurt your foot on a stone.'"

Jesus responded, "The Scriptures also say, 'You must not test the Lord your God.'"

Next the devil took him to the peak of a very high mountain and showed him all the kingdoms of the world and their glory. "I will give it all to you," he said, "if you will kneel down and worship me."

"Get out of here, Satan," Jesus told him. "For the Scriptures say,
'You must worship the Lord your God
and serve only him.'"

Then the devil went away, and angels came and took care of Jesus.

Devotional Thought

Jesus ain't no punk. Fresh out of a 40-day fast—hungry, physically weak, and alone—the enemy thought He found His opening. But even in His wilderness moment, Jesus showed unshakable strength.

The devil tried to bait Him with food. Jesus showed discipline, feasting on the Word instead. The devil tried to twist Scripture to trap Him. Jesus cut it down with the truth of God's Word— accurate, precise, unshaken. The devil dangled power, riches, and shortcuts, but Jesus didn't give any energy to those efforts. He didn't argue, bargain, or delay. Every lie got a quick, sharp rebuttal from the Word.

What makes this moment powerful is that Jesus didn't need to prove who He was. The devil kept saying, *"If you are the Son of God..."* but Jesus didn't entertain it. His identity was already settled. He is who He is—no performance required.

This is the blueprint for us. Temptation always tries to catch us when we're tired, lonely, hungry, or weak. But our real strength isn't physical—it's spiritual. And like Jesus, we can answer lies with truth, not willpower. Temptation isn't proof that God has abandoned us; it's often preparation to sharpen us. Wilderness seasons don't break us—they build us.

Jesus shows us how to fight: not with fists, but with the Word; not with ego, but with identity. And when the battle ended, angels came to care for Him. Victory always brings God's presence and restoration.

Reflection Questions

1. **How am I using God's Word when temptation hits?**

- Do I have truth stored up, ready to answer lies when they come?
- Am I letting the Word shape me daily, or only quoting it when convenient?

_____

_____

_____

_____

_____

_____

_____

2. **Do I know my identity well enough to resist manipulation?**

- Where do I feel pressured to prove my worth?
- Do I stand secure in what God has already spoken about me?

_____

_____

_____

_____

_____

_____

_____

3. **What does wilderness look like in my life—and am I walking out stronger?**

- Am I treating my wilderness as punishment, or as preparation?
- What strength is God building in me while I wait?

_____

_____

_____

_____

_____

_____

_____

_____

Prayer

Jesus,

Thank You for showing me what to do in the face of temptation. When I am weak, be strong for me. When the enemy lies, bring Your truth to my memory. Help me to be rooted in Your Word so I have a weapon ready in every battle. Teach me to stand firm in who I am in You, without needing to prove myself to anyone. Strengthen me in my wilderness seasons so I come out prepared for the next level.
Amen.

DAY 2

AUTHORITY ON DISPLAY

Scripture Reading

Mark 1:21–28 (NLT)

Jesus and His companions went to the town of Capernaum. When the Sabbath day came, He went into the synagogue and began to teach. The people were amazed at His teaching, for He taught with real authority—quite unlike the teachers of religious law.

Suddenly, a man in the synagogue who was possessed by an evil spirit cried out, "Why are You interfering with us, Jesus of Nazareth? Have You come to destroy us? I know who You are—the Holy One of God!"

But Jesus reprimanded him. "Be quiet! Come out of the man," He ordered. At that, the evil spirit screamed, threw the man into a convulsion, and then came out of him.

Amazement gripped the audience, and they began to discuss what had happened. "What sort of new teaching is this?" they asked excitedly. "It has such authority! Even evil spirits obey His orders!" The news about Jesus spread quickly throughout the entire region of Galilee.

Devotional Thought

Jesus didn't just teach the Word—He embodied authority. When He walked into the synagogue that Sabbath, He wasn't just filling time with clever words or quoting traditions like everyone else was used to. His voice carried weight because His words came from Heaven, not from human opinion. People instantly recognized the difference:

this wasn't a teacher trying to prove a point, this was the Son of God declaring truth.

Then things got real. A demon, hidden in the crowd, couldn't stay silent in His presence. Darkness gets nervous when true light shows up. The evil spirit shouted, exposing its fear: *"I know who You are!"* It knew Jesus was the Holy One of God, and it knew its time was up. Notice—Jesus didn't get rattled. He didn't call for a ritual, burn incense, or put on a show. He simply spoke: *"Be quiet. Come out."* And just like that, the man was free.

No theatrics. No hesitation. Just power.

Jesus chose to do this in the synagogue—on the Sabbath. That was bold. He wasn't worried about what the religious leaders would think or about offending tradition. He wasn't playing it safe. He put authority on display in front of everyone so there would be no question who He was.

Here's the truth: Jesus didn't back down when confronted by darkness, and neither should we. His presence calls out what's fake, what's oppressive, and what doesn't belong. And His Spirit in us gives us that same authority—not to draw attention to ourselves, but to bring freedom, clarity, and truth into the spaces we step into.

Jesus ain't no punk. He doesn't flinch when the enemy tries to bark. He speaks, and even demons have to obey. If we walk with Him, we don't need to live in fear of spiritual pressure—we walk in the authority He's already given us.

Reflection Questions

1. **Where is God calling me to speak up, lead, or teach—but I've been holding back?**

-   What's keeping you from walking in the spiritual authority Jesus has already given you?

_____

_____

_____

_____

_____

_____

_____

2. **Where have I been silent when I should've spoken truth?**

-   *Jesus never stayed quiet when it was time to confront lies. What's one situation where I chose comfort over courage— and how can I change that next time?*

_____

_____

_____

_____

_____

_____

_____

3. **When spiritual opposition shows up, how do I respond?**

- Do I shrink back in fear, or do I stand confident in Christ and confront it with His Word and His authority?

_____

_____

_____

_____

_____

_____

_____

_____

4. **What disruptive or impure voices in my life need to be silenced?**

- _Jesus didn't entertain the demon's words—He shut it down. What thoughts, influences, or even people are speaking fear, doubt, or confusion into me that I need to silence in Jesus' name?_

_____

_____

_____

_____

_____

_____

_____

_____

Prayer

Jesus,

Thank You for showing me what real authority looks like. You weren't shaken by darkness, and You never backed down in the face of opposition. Teach me to walk in that same boldness. Give me courage to speak truth, even when it's uncomfortable. Help me to silence the voices of fear, doubt, and distraction in my life and live with confidence in the authority You've given me. Let Your presence in me bring light wherever I go.

Amen.

DAY 3

HE FLIPPED MORE THAN TABLES

Scripture Reading

John 2:13–22 (NLT)

13 It was nearly time for the Jewish Passover Celebration, so Jesus went to Jerusalem. 14 In the Temple area he saw merchants selling cattle, sheep, and doves for sacrifices; he also saw dealers at tables exchanging foreign money. 15 Jesus made a whip from some ropes and chased them all out of the Temple. He drove out the sheep and cattle, scattered the money changers' coins over the floor, and turned over their tables. 16 Then going over to the people who sold doves, He told them, "Get these things out of here. Stop turning my Father's house into a marketplace!" 17 Then his disciples remembered this prophecy from the Scriptures: "Passion for God's house will consume me." 18 But the Jewish leaders demanded, "What are you doing? If God gave you authority to do this, show us a miraculous sign to prove it." 19 "All right," Jesus replied. "Destroy this temple, and in three days I will raise it up." 20 "What!" they exclaimed. "It has taken forty-six years to build this Temple, and you say you can rebuild it in three days?" 21 But when Jesus said "this temple," he meant his own body. 22 After He was raised from the dead, His disciples remembered He had said this, and they believed both the Scriptures and what Jesus had said.

Devotional Thought

When people hear the phrase *"Jesus Ain't No Punk,"* they often bring up the time He flipped tables. That moment definitely shows His boldness—but that's just one scene in a bigger story. Jesus wasn't just bold for a moment; He was bold with a mission.

Jesus didn't just walk into that temple and flip a few tables—He walked in with full authority and zero hesitation. That moment was more than just dramatic. *It was deliberate, strong, and holy. It wasn't about rage; it was about righteousness.*

Imagine walking into your church during worship or the sermon, feeling moved to go to the altar. But instead of space to meet God, you're bombarded with,
"Prayer cloths half off!"
"Get your anointing oil. It's the best stuff in town!"
"Genuine Italian leather Bibles—Get 'em while it's hot!"

Would anyone be able to focus on worship or the Word with all that chaos and noise? Absolutely not. We would likely all walk out of that church and never return. And Jesus wasn't having it either.

Jesus walked into the temple during Passover—one of the most sacred times of the year—and what did He see? A bunch of hustlers. Merchants selling livestock, vendors yelling about doves, and money changers making a profit off of worship. What was supposed to be holy had become hollow.

Jesus didn't stand by quietly. He didn't avoid confrontation to keep the peace. He made a whip. That alone should tell you this wasn't about rage—it was about righteous purpose. He drove out the distractions, flipped the tables, and declared, "Stop turning my Father's house into a marketplace!"

This wasn't out-of-control fury. This was divine authority in action. Jesus showed up with clarity, purpose, and courage. He knew what the temple was *supposed* to be—and He refused to let people twist it into something else.

And when the religious leaders challenged Him, Jesus didn't back down. He made it plain: *"Destroy this temple, and I will raise it in three days."* He wasn't just talking about a building; He was talking about His body. Even in the face of misunderstanding and resistance,

He held His ground. Why? Because Jesus knew who He was, and He wasn't about to play small for anybody.

Jesus didn't just flip tables. He flipped the whole system of compromise and spiritual laziness. He called people back to real worship, real holiness, and real courage.

He still does.

Reflection Questions

1. **What ways of thinking, habits, or compromises in my life would Jesus "flip" if He walked into my temple (my heart) today?**

   – What have I allowed to take up sacred space in my life that needs to be cleared out?

   _____

   _____

   _____

   _____

   _____

   _____

   _____

2. *Jesus told the truth even when others didn't get it. Where do I need to speak truth with boldness—even if people don't understand me at first?*

   – *Is there a place where I've been shrinking back when God is calling me to stand up?*

   _____

   _____

   _____

   _____

   _____

   _____

   _____

3. **Jesus didn't just pray about the problem—He acted. Where is God calling me to stop being passive and start taking holy action?**

   – What bold step do I need to take this week that honors God's house—starting with my own heart?

   _____

   _____

   _____

   _____

   _____

   _____

   _____

   _____

Prayer

Jesus,

Thank You for showing me what it looks like to take authority and stand on business in boldness. Help me to drive out anything in my life that may be causing me to compromise myself and even others in my life that are watching me. Show me what needs to be cleared out of my life so I can worship You fully. I want to have holy and controlled anger in the face of injustice just like You. Give me strength to flip what needs flipping—and peace to let go of what You never told me to carry.

You're not a punk and I don't want to be either.

Amen.

DAY 4

REAL RECOGNIZES REAL

Scripture Reading

Matthew 8:5–13 (NLT)

5 When Jesus returned to Capernaum, a Roman officer came and pleaded with Him, 6 "Lord, my young servant lies in bed, paralyzed and in terrible pain." 7 Jesus said, "I will come and heal him." 8 But the officer said, "Lord, I am not worthy to have You come into my home. Just say the word from where You are, and my servant will be healed. 9 I know this because I am under the authority of my superior officers, and I have authority over my soldiers. I only need to say, 'Go,' and they go, or 'Come,' and they come. And if I say to my slaves, 'Do this,' they do it." 10 When Jesus heard this, He was amazed. Turning to those who were following Him, He said, "I tell you the truth, I haven't seen faith like this in all Israel! 11 And I tell you this, that many Gentiles will come from all over the world—from east and west—and sit down with Abraham, Isaac, and Jacob at the feast in the Kingdom of Heaven. 12 But many Israelites—those for whom the Kingdom was prepared—will be thrown into outer darkness, where there will be weeping and gnashing of teeth." 13 Then Jesus said to the Roman officer, "Go back home. Because you believed, it has happened." And the young servant was healed that same hour.

Devotional Thought

Jesus walked in full authority. If He had been the soft, meek figure some paintings make Him out to be, this moment would've gone a lot differently. Jesus didn't need an entourage, special lighting, or theme music to announce Him—He just stepped into a place, and His presence was unmistakable.

So why would a Roman officer—a man with status, political clout, and military backing—approach a Jewish teacher for help?

24

Because **real recognizes real**. This officer knew what power and authority looked like, and he knew Jesus carried it on another level.

Jesus didn't hesitate to offer action: "I will come and heal him." But the officer stopped Him—not because he doubted, but because he understood. He recognized that true authority doesn't have to show up in person to make things happen. If Jesus spoke the word, that was enough.

This is the kind of faith that turns heads—even Jesus marveled at it. The man's position, nationality, and outsider status didn't matter. Jesus didn't act out of fear of Roman power; He acted out of love and compassion.

And then Jesus did something bold—He turned to the crowd and said, in essence, *"Don't think you're in just because you've got the right background. Faith is the real qualifier, and some of the people you consider outsiders will be sitting at the table while others miss out completely."*

That statement cut deep. It offended the comfortable and challenged the entitled. But that's what Jesus does—He tells the truth, even if it stings.

Jesus ain't no punk. He's bold, compassionate, unshaken by earthly power, unmatched in heavenly power, and moved by real faith. When He speaks, even sickness bows.

Reflection Questions

1. **How do I approach Jesus?**
   – Is my approach casual, or do I come to Him fully recognizing His authority like the Roman officer did?
   – How seriously do I take His authority over my life, my struggles, and my future?

   _____

   _____

   _____

   _____

   _____

   _____

   _____

   _____

2. **Do I trust His word alone?**
   – The officer didn't need proof—he believed Jesus' word was enough. Do I trust Him without demanding signs?

   _____

   _____

   _____

   _____

   _____

   _____

   _____

   _____

3. **Am I relying on my label or living in faith?**

   – The religious crowd missed it. Am I leaning on my "Christian" identity, my background, or my knowledge, instead of walking in humble, active faith?

   _____

   _____

   _____

   _____

   _____

   _____

   _____

   _____

   _____

4. **Can I handle truth from Jesus?**

   – Do I welcome His hard words, or do I filter out anything that challenges my comfort?

   _____

   _____

   _____

   _____

   _____

   _____

   _____

   _____

   _____

Prayer

Jesus,

Thank You for the authority and power You still have today. Help me step aside from pride and humble myself so Your power can freely work in my life. Give me faith that is bold, confident, and rooted in who You are—not in what I can see. Keep me from relying on labels, habits, or traditions as my safety net. I want to walk in the kind of faith You honor.
Amen.

Day 5

Dinner with Outcasts

Luke 5:27–31 (NLT)

Later, as Jesus left the town, he saw a tax collector named Levi (also called Matthew) sitting at his tax collector's booth. "Follow me and be my disciple," Jesus said to him. So Levi got up, left everything, and followed him.

Later, Levi held a banquet in his home with Jesus as the guest of honor. Many of Levi's fellow tax collectors and other guests also ate with them. But the Pharisees and their teachers of religious law complained bitterly to Jesus' disciples, "Why do you eat and drink with such scum?"

Jesus answered them, "Healthy people don't need a doctor—sick people do. I have come to call not those who think they are righteous, but those who know they are sinners and need to repent."

Devotional Thought

Jesus ain't no punk. When He called Matthew, He did it brazenly, in public, and without hesitation. He didn't wait until no one was looking, didn't pull Matthew to the side, and didn't worry about the reputation hit that came with being seen around "the rejects." He locked eyes with a man everyone else despised and said two life-changing words: "Follow Me."

That's authority without the extra fluff. That's confidence without compromise. Jesus knew exactly who He was calling and what people would say about it—and He did it anyway. Matthew's job as a tax collector made him one of the most hated men in town. To the religious elite, he was unclean, untouchable, unworthy. But to Jesus, he was chosen, valuable, and redeemable.

Notice how quickly Matthew responded. He didn't negotiate. He didn't ask for guarantees. He just *got up and left everything*. That shows the kind of authority Jesus carried—one command and everything shifted. Jesus wasn't recruiting by appealing to status or comfort; He was offering purpose and identity.

The Pharisees couldn't handle this. They weren't even brave enough to confront Jesus directly—they whispered complaints to His disciples. But Jesus wasn't fazed. He faced them head-on and made His mission crystal clear: "I came for the sick, not the self-righteous." He didn't waste energy trying to appease critics. He redirected the whole conversation toward truth, mercy, and His greater purpose.

Here's the challenge: Jesus still calls people publicly, in places we wouldn't expect, and He still steps into "dirty" spaces without flinching. He sees value where the world sees trash. He defends the rejected and invites them to His table. The question is—do we? Or do we quietly distance ourselves so we look "clean" to others?

Reflection Questions

1. *Jesus called Matthew in a public place, unapologetically - What does that say about how Jesus sees your value?*

- Are there parts of your life that make you feel disqualified (past mistakes, job, reputation)?
- What would it look like to let Jesus step into those "dirty" spaces and call you deeper?

_____

_____

_____

_____

_____

_____

_____

2. *Jesus hung out with sinners - How does this challenge your view of where He's willing to show up?*

- Who is invited into your space? Do people feel judged around you or welcomed?
- How do you respond to messy people—mercy, or distance?

_____

_____

_____

_____

_____

_____

3. *Jesus defended the rejected.*

- When was the last time you stood for mercy over performance, even when it was uncomfortable?
- Is there someone in your life who just needs presence—not fixing, not correcting—just someone to sit at their table?

_____

_____

_____

_____

_____

_____

_____

Prayer

Jesus,

Thank You for coming for me in my mess. I didn't have to be perfect for You to want me. Help me believe that the parts of my life I'm most ashamed of don't disqualify me—they're the very places You want to redeem. Give me Your eyes to see people the way You do. Teach me to sit at tables the world avoids, to stand up for the rejected, and to show mercy without hesitation.

Amen

DAY 6

BECAUSE YOU SAY SO

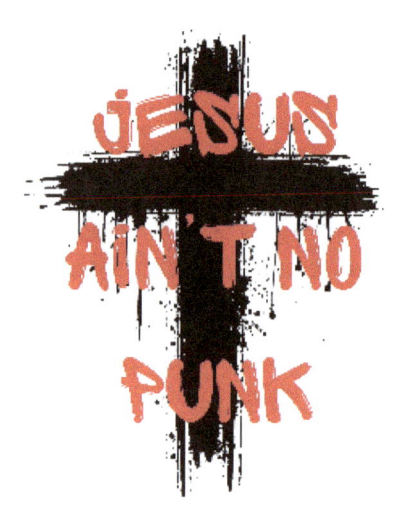

Luke 5:1–11 (NLT)

One day as Jesus was preaching on the shore of the Sea of Galilee, great crowds pressed in on him to listen to the word of God. He noticed two empty boats at the water's edge, for the fishermen had left them and were washing their nets. Stepping into one of the boats, Jesus asked Simon, its owner, to push it out into the water. So he sat in the boat and taught the crowds from there.

When he had finished speaking, he said to Simon, "Now go out where it is deeper, and let down your nets to catch some fish."

"Master," Simon replied, "we worked hard all last night and didn't catch a thing. But if you say so, I'll let the nets down again."

And this time their nets were so full of fish they began to tear! A shout for help brought their partners in the other boat, and soon both boats were filled with fish and on the verge of sinking.

When Simon Peter realized what had happened, he fell to his knees before Jesus and said, "Oh, Lord, please leave me—I'm such a sinful man." For he was awestruck by the number of fish they had caught, as were the others with him. His partners, James and John, the sons of Zebedee, were also amazed.

Jesus replied to Simon, "Don't be afraid! From now on you'll be fishing for people!"

And as soon as they landed, they left everything and followed Jesus.

Devotional Thought

Jesus ain't no punk. The way He called His first disciples showed it from the start. He didn't beg, bribe, or put on a flashy show. He simply gave a command that demanded faith—"Go deeper." That one instruction revealed both His authority and His power.

Simon had every reason to brush Jesus off. He was a professional fisherman who had just failed after an exhausting night. But something about Jesus' presence carried weight. So when Jesus told him to try again, Simon's response was, "Because You say so." That simple act of obedience turned failure into a miracle so overwhelming it nearly sank the boats.

Notice how Jesus led: He didn't belittle Simon's failure. He didn't shame him. He just called him deeper. That's power mixed with humility. That's leadership rooted in confidence, not insecurity. Jesus saw greatness in Simon when Simon only saw weakness, and He called it out.

This miracle wasn't about the fish—it was about authority. Jesus was saying, "I'm not just in control of teaching and preaching. I'm in control of creation itself. Even the fish obey Me." He wanted Simon and the others to know exactly who they were following. No wonder they dropped everything. You don't leave safety, security, and control to follow a timid leader. You leave it all for someone who commands the impossible with a word.

And here's the challenge for us: Jesus still calls us deeper. He still interrupts our comfort zones. He still challenges our human wisdom with His divine authority. The question is—will we hesitate, or will we respond with "Because You say so"?

Reflection Questions

1. **Are you staying in the shallow when Jesus is calling you to go deeper?**

- What would "going deeper" in your faith look like right now?
- Are you playing it safe spiritually because you're afraid of failing again?

_____

_____

_____

_____

_____

_____

_____

2. **Are you trusting your experience more than the authority of Jesus?**

- Where have you been relying on your own wisdom instead of obeying His voice?
- Are you willing to step out in faith even when it doesn't make sense?

_____

_____

_____

_____

_____

_____

3. **What would it look like for you to obey Jesus without hesitation?**

- Peter said, "Because You say so." What would it take for you to obey with that kind of trust?
- Could it be that your vision is too small for what God wants to do in your life?

_____

_____

_____

_____

_____

_____

_____

Prayer

Jesus,

Thank You for stepping into my world and calling me out of the shallow places. Help me to trust Your authority more than my own experience. Remove my fear, my doubt, and my hesitation. Teach me to respond like Peter—quickly, confidently, and fully—because You said so. Lead me deeper, and help me to leave everything behind to follow You without looking back.

Amen.

DAY 7

UNSHAKEN BY REJECTION

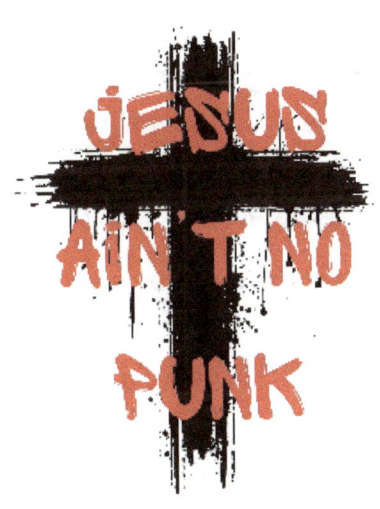

Scripture Reading

Matthew 13:53–58 (NLT)

53 When Jesus had finished telling these stories and illustrations, He left that part of the country. 54 He returned to Nazareth, His hometown. When He taught there in the synagogue, everyone was amazed and said, "Where does He get this wisdom and the power to do miracles?" 55 Then they scoffed, "He's just the carpenter's son, and we know Mary, His mother, and His brothers—James, Joseph, Simon, and Judas. 56 All His sisters live right here among us. Where did He learn all these things?" 57 And they were deeply offended and refused to believe in Him.

Then Jesus told them, "A prophet is honored everywhere except in his own hometown and among his own family." 58 And so He did only a few miracles there because of their unbelief.

Devotional Thought

Jesus knew He wasn't going to get the red-carpet welcome in His hometown. To them, He was just "that kid from up the street" or "the carpenter's son." They couldn't see past their own perception of Him. But that didn't stop Him from showing up and revealing who He truly was.

The people there missed out—not because Jesus lacked power, but because they couldn't see past familiarity. Their unbelief put a cap on what they could receive. Still, Jesus didn't let that rejection define Him or slow Him down. He didn't think, *"If my own people won't accept me, why would anyone else?"* He wasn't fishing for approval, likes, or applause.

Jesus knew exactly who He was and what He was sent to do. He kept moving forward in confidence, speaking truth, teaching with authority, and working miracles—even if some would ignore it. Their rejection wasn't His problem to fix. He offered the invitation to believe; whether they accepted it was entirely up to them.

That's the kind of confidence we're called to have—rooted in our calling, unshaken by doubt, and fearless in the face of rejection. Jesus ain't no punk, and neither should we be.

Reflection Questions

1. **Have I abandoned something God called me to** because those closest to me didn't believe in it?
   – Where do I need to pick it back up and move forward boldly, regardless of who doubts me?

   _____

   _____

   _____

   _____

   _____

   _____

   _____

   _____

2. **Am I chasing validation or walking in quiet, unshakable confidence?**
   – Where in my life do I need to stop trying to prove myself and just live out my calling?

   _____

   _____

   _____

   _____

   _____

   _____

   _____

   _____

3. **What would it look like for me to live like Jesus—steady in mission, unbothered by rejection?**

   – In what areas of my life can I start living more boldly, no matter what the naysayers think?

   _____

   _____

   _____

   _____

   _____

   _____

   _____

   _____

   _____

Prayer

Jesus,

Thank You for showing me how to walk boldly in the face of rejection. Thank You for every purpose, gift, and idea You've placed in me. Give me the strength to carry them out to completion, no matter what doubt, lack of support, or rejection I face. Help me to trust You as the One who will get me to the finish line, and keep my focus on pleasing You—not people.

Amen.

DAY 8

NO NEUTRAL GROUND

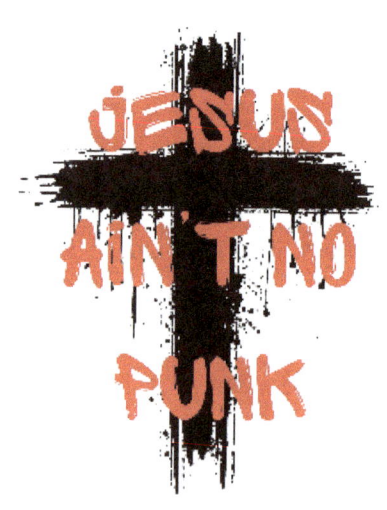

Scripture Reading

Luke 11:14–28 (NLT)

One day Jesus cast out a demon from a man who couldn't speak, and when the demon was gone, the man began to speak. The crowds were amazed, but some of them said, "No wonder he can cast out demons. He gets his power from Satan, the prince of demons."

Others, trying to test Jesus, demanded that he show them a miraculous sign from heaven to prove his authority.

He knew their thoughts, so he said, "Any kingdom divided by civil war is doomed. A family splintered by feuding will fall apart. You say I am empowered by Satan. But if Satan is divided and fighting against himself, how can his kingdom survive?

And if I am empowered by Satan, what about your own exorcists? They cast out demons, too, so they will condemn you for what you have said. But if I am casting out demons by the power of God, then the Kingdom of God has arrived among you.

For when a strong man is fully armed and guards his palace, his possessions are safe—until someone even stronger attacks and overpowers him, strips him of his weapons, and carries off his belongings.

"Anyone who isn't with me opposes me, and anyone who isn't working with me is actually working against me.

"When an evil spirit leaves a person, it goes into the desert, searching for rest. But when it finds none, it says, 'I will return to the person I came from.' So it returns and finds that its former home is all swept and in order. Then the spirit finds seven other spirits more evil than itself, and they all enter the person and live there. And so that person is worse off than before."

As he was speaking, a woman in the crowd called out, "God bless your mother—the womb from which you came, and the breasts that nursed you!"

Jesus replied, "But even more blessed are all who hear the word of God and put it into practice."

Devotional Thought

Jesus ain't no punk. Straight up, He cast out a demon like it was nothing—just another day in the life . The crowd couldn't deny the power, so the haters tried to discredit the source. Instead of celebrating freedom, they accused Him of working with Satan.

Jesus didn't let it slide. He called out their nonsensical logic on the spot. "If Satan is fighting himself, his whole house crumbles." Jesus made it clear: His authority came straight from God, and His victory over evil wasn't up for debate.

Then He drew the line: *"Whoever isn't with me is against me."* No neutral ground. No halfway faith. Either we stand with Jesus fully, or we're standing against Him.

And He didn't stop there. Jesus warned that freedom without filling leaves us vulnerable. It's not enough to "clean house"—we have to *fill* our lives with God's presence, His Word, prayer, and obedience. Empty space invites the enemy back in. Transformation is about wholeness, not surface change.

Even when a woman tried to bless His mom, Jesus redirected the praise: *true blessing is hearing God's Word and putting it into practice.* In other words—obedience is where the real power and blessing flow.

Jesus was sharp, direct, and on mission. He called foolishness for what it was, exposed lies, rejected neutrality, and pointed everyone back to obedience.

Reflection Questions

1. Do I accept what Jesus does—or am I a skeptic?

- Do I need more "signs" instead of trusting what He's already revealed?
- How often do I default to cynicism instead of discernment?

_____

_____

_____

_____

_____

_____

_____

2. Do I live fully aligned with Jesus—or am I trying to stay neutral?

- Where am I holding back, trying not to "go too far" in my faith?
- What more am I waiting for before I fully surrender and obey?

_____

_____

_____

_____

_____

_____

_____

_____

3. Am I filling my life—or just cleaning it up?

- What habits of worship, prayer, community, and obedience am I building right now?
- Is there an area I "cleaned up" but left space for old habits to return—and what do I need to burn, close, or surrender for good?

_____

_____

_____

_____

_____

_____

_____

_____

_____

_____

_____

Prayer

Jesus,

Thank You for exposing lies and challenging nonsense. Build up my discernment so I can see clearly when You're working and trust what's true. Show me the places where I've tried to stay neutral and call me into full alignment with You. Clean house in my heart—and then fill me with Your Spirit, Your Word, and obedience that keeps me free. Let my life be proof that I am fully with You.

Amen.

DAY 9

DINNER WITH HYPOCRITES

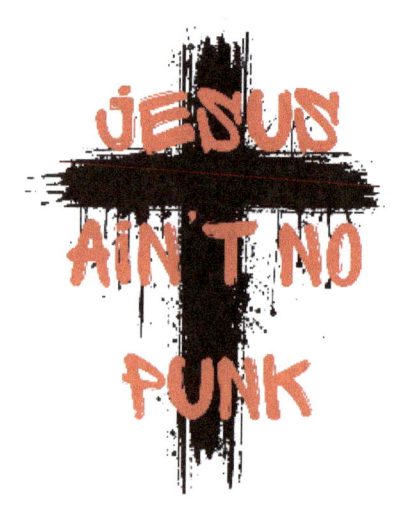

Scripture Reading

Luke 11:37–54 (NLT)

*As Jesus was speaking, one of the Pharisees invited him home for a meal. So he went in and took his place at the table.
His host was amazed to see that he sat down to eat without first performing the hand-washing ceremony required by Jewish custom.
Then the Lord said to him, "You Pharisees are so careful to clean the outside of the cup and the dish, but inside you are filthy—full of greed and wickedness! Fools! Didn't God make the inside as well as the outside?
So clean the inside by giving gifts to the poor, and you will be clean all over.

"What sorrow awaits you Pharisees! For you are careful to tithe even the tiniest income from your herb gardens, but you ignore justice and the love of God. You should tithe, yes, but do not neglect the more important things.

"What sorrow awaits you Pharisees! For you love to sit in the seats of honor in the synagogues and receive respectful greetings as you walk in the marketplaces.

"Yes, what sorrow awaits you! For you are like hidden graves in a field. People walk over them without knowing the corruption they are stepping on."

"Teacher," said an expert in religious law, "you have insulted us, too, in what you just said."

"Yes," said Jesus, "what sorrow also awaits you experts in religious law! For you crush people with unbearable religious demands, and you never lift a finger to ease the burden.

What sorrow awaits you! For you build monuments for the prophets your own ancestors killed long ago. But in fact, you stand as witnesses who agree with what your ancestors did. They killed the prophets, and you join in their crime by building the monuments! This is what God in his wisdom said about you: 'I will send prophets and apostles to them, but they will kill some and persecute the others.'

As a result, this generation will be held responsible for the murder of all God's prophets from the creation of the world—from the murder of Abel to the murder of Zechariah, who was killed between the altar and the sanctuary. Yes, it will certainly be charged against this generation.

"What sorrow awaits you experts in religious law! For you remove the key to knowledge from the people. You don't enter the Kingdom yourselves, and you prevent others from entering."

As Jesus was leaving, the teachers of religious law and the Pharisees became hostile and tried to provoke him with many questions. They wanted to trap him into saying something they could use against him.*

Devotional Thought

Jesus ain't no punk. He didn't walk into the Pharisee's house looking to impress or fit in. He came in unbothered, sat right down at the table, skipped their ceremonial handwashing rituals and started eating. That entrance alone exposed the difference between His mission and their obsession with outward appearances.

When the Pharisee questioned Him, Jesus didn't back down or apologize—He went straight to the heart of the issue. They were so focused on looking clean on the outside while ignoring the filth inside their hearts. He compared them to polished dishes that were dirty where it mattered most.

From there, Jesus dismantled their hypocrisy. They gave meticulous tithes but ignored justice and the love of God. They craved attention and honor while burdening people with heavy rules they wouldn't carry themselves. They pretended to honor the prophets while living with the same spirit that killed them. And He called out how their leadership wasn't helping people find God at all—they were gatekeeping and not sharing the keys.

Jesus' bold entrance and fearless words revealed what real holiness looks like. It isn't about rituals, image, or applause—it's about heart transformation. He showed us that God's concern is not how well we perform religion, but whether His love and justice are flowing through us from the inside out.

Reflection Questions

1. **Where in my life am I more focused on image than integrity?**

- What areas do I polish for others to see while ignoring what's happening in my heart?
- Where do I need Jesus to clean not just my habits but my motives?

_____

_____

_____

_____

_____

_____

_____

2. **Am I performing righteousness or living it?**

- Do my practices (tithing, serving, prayer) lead me into love and justice—or are they more about checking boxes?
- What's one way I can shift from religious performance to Spirit-led obedience?

_____

_____

_____

_____

_____

_____

3. Do I crave applause more than God's approval?

- Where am I seeking recognition instead of quietly serving?
- Would I still obey if no one ever noticed?

_____

_____

_____

_____

_____

_____

_____

_____

4. Am I opening doors to Jesus—or blocking them?

- Does my example draw people closer to Christ or confuse them about who He really is?
- What needs cleansing in my heart so that my life points to the real Jesus, not a fake religious version?

_____

_____

_____

_____

_____

_____

_____

_____

Prayer

Jesus,

Thank You for entering spaces without fear or compromise. Show me how to live unbothered by outward appearances and rooted in true holiness. Expose any areas of my life that look shiny on the outside but need cleansing on the inside. Transform me so that my obedience flows from love, not performance. Let my life be an open door pointing others to You.
Amen.

DAY 10

DIRTY HANDS, DIRTY HEARTS

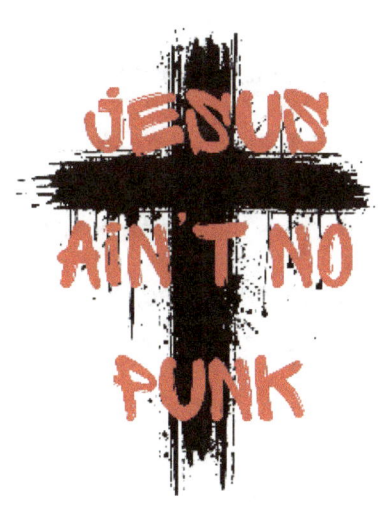

Scripture Reading

Matthew 15:1–20 (NLT)

Some Pharisees and teachers of religious law now arrived from Jerusalem to see Jesus. They asked him, "Why do your disciples disobey our age-old tradition? For they ignore our tradition of ceremonial hand washing before they eat."

*Jesus replied, "And why do you, by your traditions, violate the direct commandments of God? For instance, God says, 'Honor your father and mother,' and 'Anyone who speaks disrespectfully of father or mother must be put to death.' But you say it is all right for people to say to their parents, 'Sorry, I can't help you. For I have vowed to give to God what I would have given to you.' In this way, you say they don't need to honor their parents. And so you cancel the word of God for the sake of your own tradition. You hypocrites! Isaiah was right when he prophesied about you, for he wrote,

'These people honor me with their lips,
    but their hearts are far from me.
Their worship is a farce,
    for they teach man-made ideas as commands from God.'"*

Then Jesus called to the crowd to come and hear. "Listen," he said, "and try to understand. It's not what goes into your mouth that defiles you; you are defiled by the words that come out of your mouth."

Then the disciples came to him and asked, "Do you realize you offended the Pharisees by what you just said?"

Jesus replied, "Every plant not planted by my heavenly Father will be uprooted, so ignore them. They are blind guides leading the blind, and if one blind person guides another, they will both fall into a ditch."

Then Peter said to Jesus, "Explain to us the parable that says people aren't defiled by what they eat."

"Don't you understand yet?" Jesus asked. "Anything you eat passes through the stomach and then goes into the sewer. But the words you speak come from the heart—that's what defiles you. For from the heart come evil thoughts, murder, adultery, all sexual immorality, theft, lying, and slander. These are what defile you. Eating with unwashed hands will never defile you."

Devotional Thought

When the Pharisees showed up trying to flex tradition over truth, Jesus cut through their show like a blade. They wanted to talk about dirty hands, but Jesus flipped it—pointing straight to dirty hearts. He called out their hypocrisy right in their faces and didn't water it down. The same leaders who built their reputations on "knowing God's law" were actually bending it to serve themselves.

Instead of debating in circles, Jesus went to the root: it's not about appearances—it's about the heart. He didn't waste energy trying to impress or avoid offending. He exposed their obsession with performance and showed that real holiness flows from inside-out transformation.

Notice how Jesus shifted attention from the Pharisees to the people showing that he had no cares to give for the nonsense. He refused to stay trapped in a debate that only fed pride and posturing. He dropped truth for the crowd: it's not about what goes in your mouth but what comes out of it. That's kingdom teaching. That's freedom. That's power.

And when His disciples got nervous about how offensive He sounded, Jesus didn't soften the message. He went harder: "Leave them. They're blind guides." Translation—don't waste your time chasing approval from people who don't even see clearly.

Jesus shows us that truth doesn't bend to tradition, and boldness doesn't bow to criticism. Real faith is deeper than surface rules—it's about heart change.

Reflection Questions

1. **Where do I see religious or cultural "rules" today that put image over substance?**

- What traditions, expectations, or habits have I elevated above God's actual commands?
- Am I more concerned with "looking spiritual" than truly living connected to Jesus?

_____

_____

_____

_____

_____

_____

_____

2. **When critics challenge my faith choices, how do I respond?**

- Do I react out of insecurity, fear of rejection, or people-pleasing?
- Where do I need to rest in God's truth and let Him, not tradition, set the standard?

- _____

_____

_____

_____

_____

_____

_____

3. "What comes out of the mouth comes from the heart."

- If I reviewed my words lately—conversations, texts, posts, or comment sections—what would they reveal about my heart?
- Where do I need Jesus to cleanse my inner life so that my words line up with His truth?

_____

_____

_____

_____

_____

_____

_____

4. How do I handle offense?

- When Jesus' truth convicts me, do I dismiss it like the Pharisees or let it transform me?

_____

_____

_____

_____

_____

_____

_____

_____

Prayer

Jesus,

Thank You for showing me what really matters—my heart, not my image. Expose every place where I've been more focused on tradition, performance, or approval than on truth. Transform my heart so that what flows out of me—my words, my actions, my choices— honors You. Give me boldness to stand on truth, even when it offends comfort zones. Keep me close to Your voice and far from empty show.
Amen.

DAY 11

BOLD IN THE FACE OF HYPOCRISY

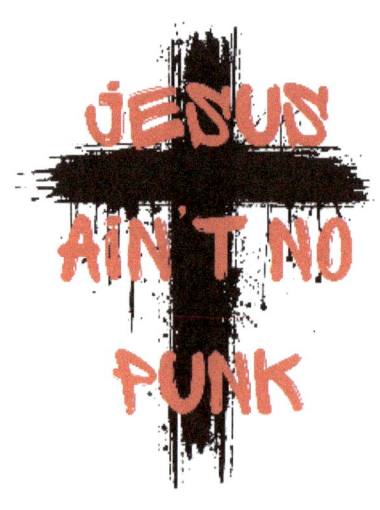

Scripture Reading

Luke 13:10–17 (NLT)

10 One Sabbath day as Jesus was teaching in a synagogue, 11 He saw a woman who had been crippled by an evil spirit. She had been bent double for eighteen years and was unable to stand up straight. 12 When Jesus saw her, He called her over and said, "Dear woman, you are healed of your sickness!" 13 Then He touched her, and instantly she could stand straight. How she praised God! 14 But the leader in charge of the synagogue was indignant that Jesus had healed her on the Sabbath day. "There are six days of the week for working," he said to the crowd. "Come on those days to be healed, not on the Sabbath." 15 But the Lord replied, "You hypocrites! Each of you works on the Sabbath day! Don't you untie your ox or your donkey from its stall on the Sabbath and lead it out for water? 16 This dear woman, a daughter of Abraham, has been held in bondage by Satan for eighteen years. Isn't it right that she be released, even on the Sabbath?" 17 This shamed His enemies, but all the people rejoiced at the wonderful things He did.

Devotional Thought

Jesus brought nuance and context to the Law with full confidence, redefining what it really meant. He didn't shrink back in fear or soften His words to keep the Pharisees happy. He stood firm in goodness and truth, and He wasn't afraid to call out hypocrisy when He saw it.

When the religious leaders confronted Him, Jesus didn't hide or sidestep the issue. His response—His *clap back*—came with full knowledge of Scripture and full authority. While the Pharisees were obsessed with rules and traditions, Jesus made it clear: *He is greater than the entire system they had built their lives around.*

This healing was not done in private. Jesus didn't wait for a "less controversial" time, and He didn't take the woman to a back room to avoid making a scene. He healed her right there, in the synagogue, on the Sabbath, in front of everyone—including His opposition.

And His words cut straight through their hypocrisy: *You'll untie an animal to give it water on the Sabbath, but you have a problem with Me freeing a daughter of Abraham from eighteen years of suffering?* The crowd rejoiced. The religious leaders had nothing to say.

Jesus knew healing her would only add fuel to the fire for those plotting against Him, but He did it anyway. Nothing soft about it. Jesus ain't no punk—He's bold, uncompromising in truth, and moved by compassion over man-made rules.

Reflection Questions

1. **How does Jesus' boldness challenge me to speak** truth in conflict?
   – Have I stayed quiet to avoid confrontation?
   – What am I afraid of losing or facing if I speak up?

   _____

   _____

   _____

   _____

   _____

   _____

   _____

2. **Do I prioritize compassion over rules?**
   – Have I ever let tradition, appearance, or expectation outweigh love and grace?
   – Who in my life right now needs compassion instead of judgment?

   _____

   _____

   _____

   _____

   _____

   _____

   _____

3. **When was the last time I boldly stood for truth?**
   – What happened as a result?
   – Did I hold back? If so, why?

_____

_____

_____

_____

_____

_____

_____

_____

Prayer

Jesus,

Thank You for showing me that truth and compassion go hand in hand. Give me courage to stand firm when it's easier to stay silent. Help me to see people the way You see them—valuable, worthy of grace, and not bound by rules that miss the heart of God. Teach me to speak boldly, love deeply, and act with conviction, even when it's uncomfortable. Let my words and actions reflect the fearless authority You carried.

Amen.

Day 12

Storm Stopper

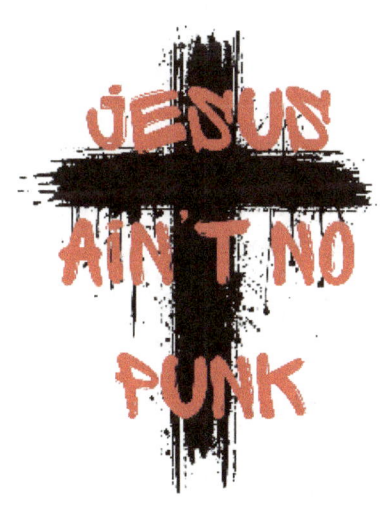

Scripture Reading

Mark 4:35–41 (NLT)

35 As evening came, Jesus said to His disciples, "Let's cross to the other side of the lake." 36 So they took Jesus in the boat and started out, leaving the crowds behind (although other boats followed). 37 But soon a fierce storm came up. High waves were breaking into the boat, and it began to fill with water. 38 Jesus was sleeping at the back of the boat with His head on a cushion. The disciples woke Him up, shouting, "Teacher, don't You care that we're going to drown?"

39 When Jesus woke up, He rebuked the wind and said to the waves, "Silence! Be still!" Suddenly the wind stopped, and there was a great calm. 40 Then He asked them, "Why are you afraid? Do you still have no faith?" 41 The disciples were absolutely terrified. "Who is this man?" they asked each other. "Even the wind and waves obey Him!"

Devotional Thought

Jesus wasn't just in the storm—He was asleep in it. And not just barely dozing—Mark makes sure to tell us He had a pillow. That's comfort. That's confidence. That's a complete lack of panic while everyone else was losing their minds, convinced the boat was going under.

Then, in one of the most anti-punk moves ever recorded, Jesus gets up and talks to the storm like it's an unruly child. *"Silence! Be still!"* And just like that, the storm obeys. All authority. All power. No theatrics—just results.

But Jesus didn't stop there. He looked His disciples in the eye and asked them why they were so afraid. He challenged their faith—not to shame them, but to push them to remember His track record and trust His presence. They had just witnessed something so wild that they ended up more scared of Jesus' power than they were of the storm.

Here's the truth: Jesus doesn't just ride along in your storms—He commands them. And sometimes, He's so unbothered by the chaos that it makes you wonder if you're panicking over something that's already under His control.

Jesus ain't no punk—He sleeps through storms, speaks to the wind, and challenges us to believe that if He's in the boat, we're not going under.

Reflection Questions

1. **Do I trust Jesus enough to carry me through storms and uncomfortable seasons?**

   – What has Jesus told me to do that I'm still holding back on because the outcome feels unclear or risky?

   _____

   _____

   _____

   _____

   _____

   _____

   _____

   _____

2. **When life starts "life-ing" too much, how do I respond?**

   – Do I panic, complain, isolate, or lash out—or do I run to Jesus?

   – Am I speaking truth to my storm, or letting my storm speak fear into me?

   _____

   _____

   _____

   _____

   _____

   _____

   _____

   _____

3. **Am I forgetting the power that's riding with me?**

   – What storm am I giving more power to than Jesus?

_____

_____

_____

_____

_____

_____

_____

_____

_____

_____

Prayer

Jesus,

Thank You for being with me—not just in the calm, but in the middle of every storm I face. Help me to remember that Your presence means I'm not in danger of sinking, even when the waves feel overwhelming. Teach me to speak Your authority over fear, doubt, and chaos. And when I can't see the outcome, help me to rest in the truth that the One who commands the wind and waves is right here with me.

Amen.

DAY 13

NO CODE SWITCHING

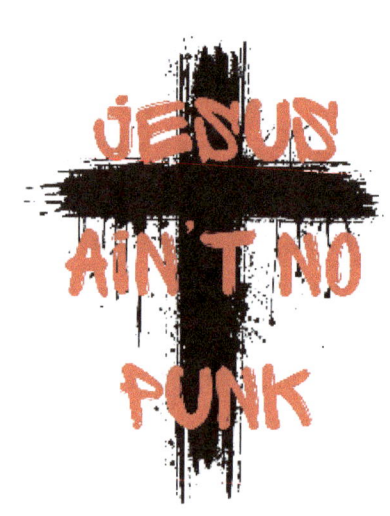

Luke 7:36–50 (NLT)

One of the Pharisees asked Jesus to have dinner with him, so Jesus went to his home and sat down to eat. When a certain immoral woman from that city heard he was eating there, she brought a beautiful alabaster jar filled with expensive perfume. Then she knelt behind him at his feet, weeping. Her tears fell on his feet, and she wiped them off with her hair. Then she kept kissing his feet and putting perfume on them.

When the Pharisee who had invited him saw this, he said to himself, "If this man were a prophet, he would know what kind of woman is touching him. She's a sinner!"

Then Jesus answered his thoughts. "Simon," he said to the Pharisee, "I have something to say to you."

"Go ahead, Teacher," Simon replied.

Then Jesus told him this story: "A man loaned money to two people—500 pieces of silver to one and 50 pieces to the other. But neither of them could repay him, so he kindly forgave them both, canceling their debts. Who do you suppose loved him more after that?"

Simon answered, "I suppose the one for whom he canceled the larger debt."

"That's right," Jesus said. Then he turned to the woman and said to Simon, "Look at this woman kneeling here. When I entered your home, you didn't offer me water to wash the dust from my feet, but she has washed them with her tears and wiped them with her hair. You didn't greet me with a kiss, but from the time I first came in, she has not stopped kissing my feet. You neglected the courtesy of olive

oil to anoint my head, but she has anointed my feet with rare perfume.

"I tell you, her sins—and they are many—have been forgiven, so she has shown me much love. But a person who is forgiven little shows only little love." Then Jesus said to the woman, "Your sins are forgiven."

The men at the table said among themselves, "Who is this man, that he goes around forgiving sins?"

And Jesus said to the woman, "Your faith has saved you; go in peace."

Devotional Thought

Jesus ain't no punk. He didn't change up His identity based on the room He was in or the people around Him. No code switching. He was the same Jesus in a Pharisee's house as He was in the streets. Confident, consistent, and unshaken.

When the woman labeled as "dirty" walked in, Jesus didn't flip out. He didn't push her away to keep His image clean. He didn't let Simon's reputation or judgment define how He treated her. He welcomed her tears, her sacrifice, her messy, broken worship. Where others saw scandal, He saw surrender. Where others whispered shame, He lifted her up with honor.

Notice this: Jesus wasn't intimidated by Simon either. He sat at the table of a man who despised Him and might've been setting a trap, but He came in calm and sure of Himself. He didn't bow to social pressure. He didn't fear labels. He knew who He was and who He came for.

And when Simon silently judged, Jesus responded not to his words but to his *thoughts*. That's power. He didn't explode in anger or humiliate him, but instead told a story sharp enough to slice through Simon's pride. Then He flipped the spotlight—contrasting Simon's cold hospitality with the woman's passionate devotion. Jesus showed that the real difference wasn't status, but love. The Pharisee had religion, but she had worship.

This moment shows us what courage looks like: Jesus honored a broken woman in public, defended her against religious scorn, and declared her forgiven—boldly, unapologetically, without needing approval. That's real leadership. That's mercy with authority. That's why Jesus ain't no punk.

Reflection Questions

1. **When Jesus comes to dine, am I more like Simon or the woman?**

- Do I try to impress Jesus with outward appearances, or am I willing to be real and vulnerable?
- Am I more concerned with looking "good" or with being forgiven and transformed?

_____

_____

_____

_____

_____

_____

_____

2. **Do I give my all like the woman, or am I holding back?**

- Am I willing to move past shame and pour myself out in worship?
- Do I value His forgiveness over maintaining my reputation?

_____

_____

_____

_____

_____

_____

_____

3. **In a culture obsessed with labels and shame, do I follow the crowd or follow Jesus?**

- Do I add to someone's shame, or do I cover with grace?
- Where is God teaching me to live with mercy, humility, and courage—even when it goes against the grain?

_____

_____

_____

_____

_____

_____

_____

_____

Prayer

Jesus,

Thank You for handling me with love even when I feel ashamed or unworthy. Help me to stop hiding behind appearances and pride. Teach me to bring my whole self to You, the messy and the broken, and trust You with it all. Give me courage to see others through Your eyes, to defend the broken, and to choose mercy over judgment. Thank You for always seeing my heart above my actions.
Amen.

DAY 14

UNTOUCHABLE POWER, UNSTOPPABLE PRESENCE

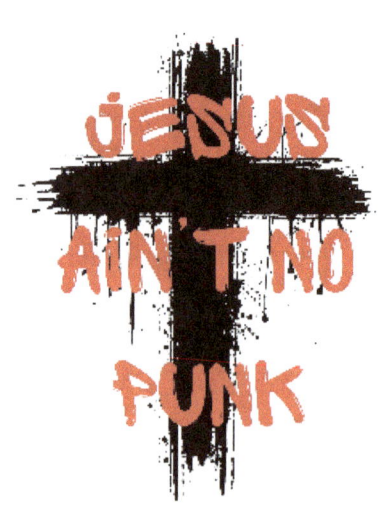

Scripture Reading

Luke 8:40–56 (NLT)

On the other side of the lake the crowds welcomed Jesus, because they had been waiting for him. Then a man named Jairus, a leader of the local synagogue, came and fell at Jesus' feet, pleading with him to come home with him. His only daughter, who was about twelve years old, was dying. As Jesus went with him, he was surrounded by the crowds.

A woman in the crowd had suffered for twelve years with constant bleeding, and she could find no cure. Coming up behind Jesus, she touched the fringe of his robe. Immediately, the bleeding stopped.

"Who touched me?" Jesus asked. Everyone denied it, and Peter said, "Master, this whole crowd is pressing up against you."

But Jesus said, "Someone deliberately touched me, for I felt healing power go out from me."

When the woman realized that she could not stay hidden, she began to tremble and fell to her knees in front of him. The whole crowd heard her explain why she had touched him and that she had been immediately healed.

"Daughter," he said to her, "your faith has made you well. Go in peace."

While he was still speaking to her, a messenger arrived from the home of Jairus, the leader of the synagogue. He told him, "Your daughter is dead. There's no use troubling the Teacher now."

But when Jesus heard what had happened, he said to Jairus, "Don't be afraid. Just have faith, and she will be healed."

When they arrived at the house, Jesus wouldn't let anyone go in with him except Peter, John, James, and the little girl's father and mother. The house was filled with people weeping and wailing, but he said, "Stop the weeping! She isn't dead; she's only asleep."

But the crowd laughed at him because they all knew she had died. Then Jesus took her by the hand and said in a loud voice, "My child, get up!"

And at that moment her life returned, and she immediately stood up! Then Jesus told them to give her something to eat. Her parents were overwhelmed, but Jesus insisted that they not tell anyone what had happened.

Devotional Thought

Jesus' presence carried so much authority that crowds formed just off His reputation. No marketing, no promotion—just the undeniable weight of who He was. People waited because they knew that when He showed up, things shifted.

The woman with the issue of blood knew this. She wasn't supposed to even be there—her condition made her "unclean" and excluded. But she had the kind of faith that said, *"If I can just touch the edge of His robe, that's enough."* And it was. Power flowed from Him without her even asking for permission. That's how strong His presence was.

And here's what makes Jesus different: when she came forward trembling, expecting judgment or rejection, He didn't shame her. He honored her faith. Publicly. He called her *daughter*. He gave her more than healing—He gave her wholeness and dignity back.

But He didn't stop there. He was already on His way to heal Jairus' daughter, and even when the word came that she had died, Jesus didn't hesitate. He didn't tap out like a punk and say, *"Well, I tried."* He went all the way. He walked past the mockery, pushed past the noise, cleared the room, and raised her up. Death itself couldn't stop Him.

Jesus doesn't rush. He isn't bound by our timelines. The delay for Jairus felt devastating, but Jesus showed that His timing is always perfect. He stopped for the invisible, restored her publicly, then went to a grieving family and turned mourning into joy. He showed power that is untouchable and presence that is unstoppable.

Reflection Questions

1. **Where have I settled for quiet suffering instead of bold faith?**

- Am I holding something in silence that Jesus is inviting me to bring forward?
- What fear—rejection, disappointment, embarrassment—is keeping me from reaching for Him openly?

_____

_____

_____

_____

_____

_____

2. **How do I respond when Jesus doesn't move at my pace?**

- Can I trust His timing even when the situation feels urgent?
- Do I try to control the outcome, or can I rest in His perfect track record?

_____

_____

_____

_____

_____

_____

_____

3. **Where am I tempted to quit just because it looks "dead"?**

- Is there a dream, relationship, or prayer I've buried too early?
- Have I started writing a eulogy while Jesus is still writing the story?

_____

_____

_____

_____

_____

_____

_____

_____

Prayer

Jesus,

Thank You that no sickness, delay, or even death can stop You. Forgive me for the times I've stayed silent in my suffering instead of reaching for You. Teach me to trust Your timing when I feel rushed or afraid. Help me to believe that no situation is too far gone for You to revive. Thank You for seeing me when I feel invisible, for restoring dignity, and for speaking life where I only see loss.

Amen.

DAY 15

NO LOOKING BACK

Scripture Reading

Luke 9:57–62 (NLT)

As they were walking along, someone said to Jesus, "I will follow you wherever you go."

But Jesus replied, "Foxes have dens to live in, and birds have nests, but the Son of Man has no place even to lay his head."

He said to another person, "Come, follow me." The man agreed, but he said, "Lord, first let me return home and bury my father."

But Jesus told him, "Let the spiritually dead bury their own dead! Your duty is to go and preach about the Kingdom of God."

Another said, "Yes, Lord, I will follow you, but first let me say good-bye to my family."

But Jesus told him, "Anyone who puts a hand to the plow and then looks back is not fit for the Kingdom of God."

Devotional Thought

Jesus ain't no punk. His whole life was a bold example of what it meant to live with unshakable trust in the Father. He was homeless, no nest, no pillow to call His own—yet He was never lacking. He lived as a nomad, fully dependent, showing that provision comes from God, not comfort or status.

When people came with half-hearted commitments or excuses, Jesus didn't sugarcoat the reality. He had no tolerance for lip service and laid it out straight: following Him was going to cost everything.

No "but first." No looking back. When God calls, delay is disobedience.

Jesus wasn't rude, but He was raw and real. He wanted His disciples to understand the urgency of the Kingdom. This wasn't about vibes or appearances—it was about focus, obedience, and surrender. He knew that if you're holding on to the past, you're not ready for the future He's calling you into. Looking back at what He's called you out of shows divided loyalty, and divided loyalty can't plow the ground for His Kingdom.

The truth is, Jesus doesn't want casual fans. He wants committed followers. People willing to give Him first place, with no conditions attached. He's after obedience, not convenience. If He didn't cower at hardship, neither can we.

Reflection Questions

1. **When Jesus calls, do I follow or do I have a "but first"?**

- What am I holding on to, claiming I need to handle before fully saying yes to Him?
- Am I delaying obedience with "good" excuses?

_____

_____

_____

_____

_____

_____

_____

2. **Do I have one hand on the job and one eye on the past?**

- What parts of my old life do I secretly long for?
- Am I romanticizing what I left behind instead of fully embracing what's ahead?

_____

_____

_____

_____

_____

_____

_____

_____

3. **Do I want the real life with Jesus, or just the vibe that comes with Him?**

- Do I follow only when it feels good, or am I ready to stay when it costs me something?
- When sacrifice is required, do I stay committed or tap out?

_____

_____

_____

_____

_____

_____

_____

_____

Prayer

Jesus,

Thank You for calling me. Help me to obey right away—not with delay, not with excuses, but with full surrender. Teach me to keep You first and to stop looking back at what You've already freed me from. Give me courage to walk this road with focus and boldness. Jesus, You ain't no punk, and neither am I—I want to walk that out every day.
Amen.

DAY 16

SENT WITH POWER

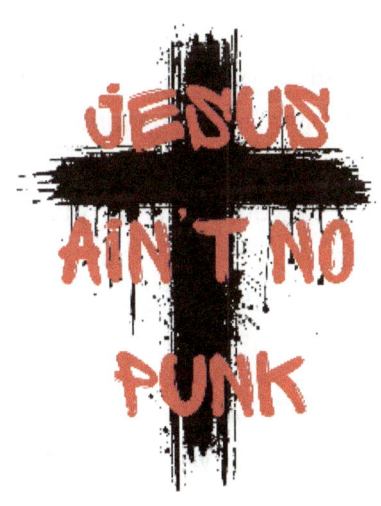

Scripture Reading

Luke 10:1–20 (NLT)

The Lord now chose seventy-two other disciples and sent them ahead in pairs to all the towns and places he planned to visit. These were his instructions to them: "The harvest is great, but the workers are few. So pray to the Lord who is in charge of the harvest; ask him to send more workers into his fields. Now go, and remember that I am sending you out as lambs among wolves. Don't take any money with you, nor a traveler's bag, nor an extra pair of sandals. And don't stop to greet anyone on the road.

Whenever you enter someone's home, first say, 'May God's peace be on this house.' If those who live there are peaceful, the blessing will stand; if they are not, the blessing will return to you. Don't move around from home to home. Stay in one place, eating and drinking what they provide. Don't hesitate to accept hospitality, because those who work deserve their pay.

If you enter a town and it welcomes you, eat whatever is set before you. Heal the sick, and tell them, 'The Kingdom of God is near you now.' But if a town refuses to welcome you, go out into its streets and say, 'We wipe even the dust of your town from our feet to show that we have abandoned you to your fate. And know this—the Kingdom of God is near!' I assure you, even wicked Sodom will be better off than such a town on judgment day.

What sorrow awaits you, Korazin and Bethsaida! For if the miracles I did in you had been done in wicked Tyre and Sidon, their people would have repented of their sins long ago, clothing themselves in burlap and throwing ashes on their heads to show their remorse. Yes, Tyre and Sidon will be better off on judgment day than you. And you people of Capernaum, will you be honored in heaven? No, you will go down to the place of the dead."

Then he said to the disciples, "Anyone who accepts your message is also accepting me. And anyone who rejects you is rejecting me. And anyone who rejects me is rejecting God, who sent me."

When the seventy-two disciples returned, they joyfully reported to him, "Lord, even the demons obey us when we use your name!"

"Yes," he told them, "I saw Satan fall from heaven like lightning! Look, I have given you authority over all the power of the enemy, and you can walk among snakes and scorpions and crush them. Nothing will injure you. But don't rejoice because evil spirits obey you; rejoice because your names are registered in heaven."

Devotional Thought

Jesus ain't no punk—He's the ultimate BOSS. Not only did He roll with the 12, but He had a whole squad of 72 ready to move. He didn't hoard the spotlight or try to do it all Himself. Like the best CEO, He delegated, empowered, and sent people out with authority and direction. He wasn't vague, He was clear. He wasn't nervous, He was confident. He wasn't micromanaging, He was trusting.

Jesus sent them out in pairs—no one had to walk alone. That's leadership with strategy: accountability, encouragement, and strength in numbers. He trained them to travel light, stay focused, and not get caught up in distractions. He didn't sugarcoat the risks. He told them flat out: some people will reject you. And that's okay. Don't waste energy where hearts are closed—move on and keep working the mission.

Like a real boss, He not only gave His disciples authority but also reminded them of the real why. Yes, demons fled when they spoke His name. Yes, miracles happened. But Jesus kept their egos in check: *don't celebrate your power—celebrate that your name is written in heaven.*

Jesus was intentional, strategic, humble, and mission-driven. He didn't just talk vision; He equipped people to live it out. That's Kingdom leadership. And He still sends us the same way: light, focused, bold, and rooted in Him.

Reflection Questions

1. **Am I living like someone appointed, or just wandering through life waiting for a sign?**

- Where has Jesus already sent me, and am I moving with urgency or sitting back with excuses?
- Who am I mentoring, equipping, or sending out—or am I trying to carry the mission alone?

_____

_____

_____

_____

_____

_____

2. **What baggage (emotional, relational, material) is slowing me down from God's work?**

- Am I so busy chasing "better conditions" that I'm missing my assignment right where I am?
- Do I trust God to provide, or am I hustling for my own bag instead of His harvest?

_____

_____

_____

_____

_____

_____

3. **Am I leading like Jesus—bold, strategic, humble—or playing it safe to keep people comfortable?**

- Do I walk in spiritual authority or live like I'm spiritually broke?
- Am I just talking about God, or am I demonstrating His power in how I live, serve, and show up?

_____

_____

_____

_____

_____

_____

_____

_____

Prayer

Jesus,

Thank You for being the perfect leader. Thank You for showing me that Kingdom work isn't solo—it's strategic, bold, and Spirit-powered. Help me to obey when You send me, to travel light, and to stay focused on the mission instead of distractions. Teach me to mentor, equip, and raise others like You did. Keep my heart humble so I celebrate not the power You give, but the fact that my name is written in heaven.

Amen.

DAY 17

SET THE WORLD ON FIRE

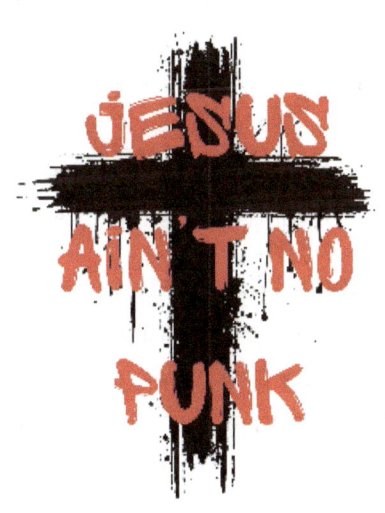

Scripture Reading

Luke 12:49–59 (NLT)

*"I have come to set the world on fire, and I wish it were already burning!

I have a terrible baptism of suffering ahead of me, and I am under a heavy burden until it is accomplished.

Do you think I have come to bring peace to the earth? No, I have come to divide people against each other!

From now on families will be split apart, three in favor of me, and two against—or two in favor and three against.

'Father will be divided against son and son against father;

mother against daughter and daughter against mother;

and mother-in-law against daughter-in-law and daughter-in-law against mother-in-law.'"

Then Jesus turned to the crowd and said, "When you see clouds beginning to form in the west, you say, 'Here comes a shower.' And you are right.

When the south wind blows, you say, 'Today will be a scorcher.' And it is.

You fools! You know how to interpret the weather signs of the earth and sky, but you don't know how to interpret the present times.

"Why can't you decide for yourselves what is right? When you are on the way to court with your accuser, try to settle the matter before you get there. Otherwise, your accuser may drag you before the judge, who will hand you over to an officer, who will throw you into prison. And if that happens, you won't be free again until you have paid the very last penny."*

Devotional Thought

*Jesus doesn't tiptoe into this moment. He comes in blazing—literally—announcing that He came to **set the world on fire.** There's no soft entry, no polite buildup, just raw urgency. He lets His followers know He isn't here for surface-level peace but for a refining fire that purifies, exposes, and transforms.*

Jesus makes it clear that following Him won't keep everyone comfortable. Truth divides before it unites. Even families would split because of Him. And while His words sound harsh, they were filled with love because He refused to let His people stay blind, lukewarm, or asleep to eternal realities.

He exposed the crowd's spiritual laziness. They could predict the weather, yet they ignored the obvious signs of God's movement right in front of them. They had the knowledge but chose not to act on it. Jesus pressed them to settle things now—make peace with God, walk in obedience—before it was too late.

This audacious entrance, these sharp words, all pointed to urgency. Jesus was heading toward His suffering, crucifixion, and resurrection, so He called His followers to wake up, respond, and not delay. His fire is not for destruction but for refining—burning away complacency, compromise, and comfort so that we can stand fully alive in Him.

Reflection Questions

1. **Where am I resisting the fire Jesus wants to bring into my life?**

- What habits, comforts, or hidden areas am I protecting from His refining work?
- Are there truths I've been avoiding because they'll cost me something?

_____

_____

_____

_____

_____

_____

_____

2. **Am I ready for the division that comes with following Jesus boldly?**

- Do I water down truth to keep peace with people?
- Where have I compromised my faith to avoid rejection or tension?

_____

_____

_____

_____

_____

_____

_____

3. **Can I recognize what God is doing in this present moment?**

- Am I spiritually awake or just coasting in religious autopilot?
- What signs of His work around me am I ignoring?

_____

_____

_____

_____

_____

_____

_____

_____

4. **Am I living like I have time—or like judgment is real and urgent?**

- Have I delayed obedience, reconciliation, or repentance, assuming I'll "get right later"?
- What's the one thing I keep pushing off that Jesus is telling me to face today?

_____

_____

_____

_____

_____

_____

Prayer

Jesus,

Thank You for bringing the fire. Don't let me live blind, distracted, or spiritually asleep. Burn away the parts of me that resist You, even when it costs me relationships, comfort, or approval. Help me to see clearly what You are doing right now and give me urgency to respond in obedience today. I don't want to live this life like it's a game—I want to live fully awake in You.

Amen.

Day 18

THE CORNERSTONE THEY COULDN'T CRUSH

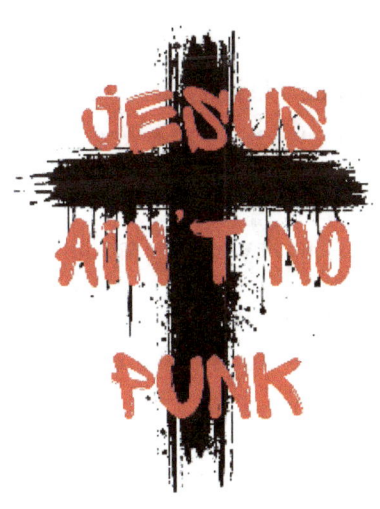

Scripture Reading

Matthew 21:33–46 (NLT)

"Now listen to another story. A certain landowner planted a vineyard, built a wall around it, dug a pit for pressing out the grape juice, and built a lookout tower. Then he leased the vineyard to tenant farmers and moved to another country. At the time of the grape harvest, he sent his servants to collect his share of the crop. But the farmers grabbed his servants, beat one, killed one, and stoned another. So the landowner sent a larger group of his servants to collect for him, but the results were the same. Finally, the owner sent his son, thinking, 'Surely they will respect my son.'

But when the tenant farmers saw his son coming, they said to one another, 'Here comes the heir to this estate. Come on, let's kill him and get the estate for ourselves!' So they grabbed him, dragged him out of the vineyard, and murdered him.

"When the owner of the vineyard returns," Jesus asked, "what do you think he will do to those farmers?"

The religious leaders replied, "He will put the wicked men to a horrible death and lease the vineyard to others who will give him his share of the crop after each harvest."

*Then Jesus asked them, "Didn't you ever read this in the Scriptures?

'The stone that the builders rejected
    has now become the cornerstone.
This is the Lord's doing,
    and it is wonderful to see.'

I tell you, the Kingdom of God will be taken away from you and given to a nation that will produce the proper fruit. Anyone who stumbles over that stone will be broken to pieces, and it will crush anyone it falls on."*

When the leading priests and Pharisees heard this parable, they realized he was telling the story against them—they were the wicked farmers. They wanted to arrest him, but they were afraid of the crowds, who considered Jesus to be a prophet.

Devotional Thought

In this parable, Jesus wasn't just telling a story—He was calling out corruption, abuse of power, and hard hearts right to the faces of the religious elite. He painted a picture of unfaithful tenants who thought they could hijack what didn't belong to them. At first, the leaders didn't catch on, but once they realized He was talking about them, they were hot.

Notice the brilliance: Jesus had them answer His own question. They literally condemned themselves with their own words before they even realized what was happening. That's boldness. That's wisdom. That's fearless truth-telling.

But Jesus went even deeper—He exposed their plot to kill Him before they even acted on it. He wasn't intimidated. He knew exactly what they were planning and declared ahead of time that God's plan would still stand. They might reject Him, but He was the cornerstone—the very foundation everything else would be built on. Their rejection couldn't stop His mission; it would only prove it.

This parable isn't just about them—it's about us too. Are we living like faithful stewards of what God has trusted us with, or are we clinging to control like greedy tenants, trying to edge out the true Owner? Do we reject the "servants" God sends into our lives—messages of correction, accountability, or truth—because they're uncomfortable? Jesus reminds us that God's Kingdom isn't built on appearances, tradition, or comfort. It's built on Him—the cornerstone.

Reflection Questions

1. **Am I living like a faithful steward or a power-hungry tenant?**

- Have I claimed ownership over things God has only entrusted to me?
- Am I using my gifts, resources, and influence for His glory, or am I taking credit for myself?

_____

_____

_____

_____

_____

_____

2. **Who are the God-sent servants I've resisted or ignored?**

- Has God sent people into my life with correction, wisdom, or accountability that I brushed off?
- What "messages" have I rejected because they didn't look or sound the way I wanted?

_____

_____

_____

_____

_____

_____

3. How do I respond when my authority or comfort is challenged?

- Do I get defensive when truth hits close to home, or do I humble myself and let God work?
- Where am I protecting my comfort instead of pursuing His Kingdom?

_____

_____

_____

_____

_____

_____

_____

_____

Prayer

Jesus,

Thank You for being the cornerstone that cannot be rejected or removed. Thank You for loving me enough to challenge me in areas where I resist surrender. Expose where I've acted like a greedy tenant, trying to take ownership of what belongs to You. Give me humility to receive Your correction and courage to release control. Build my life fully on You—the foundation that never cracks, never shifts, and never fails.

Amen.

DAY 19

THE KING WHO COMMANDS the STREETS

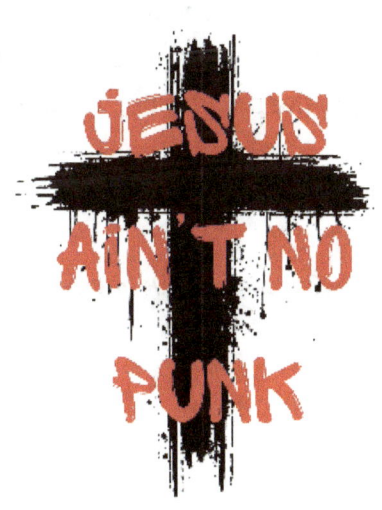

Scripture Reading

Mark 11:1–10 (NLT)

As Jesus and his disciples approached Jerusalem, they came to the towns of Bethphage and Bethany on the Mount of Olives. Jesus sent two of them on ahead.

"Go into that village over there," he told them. "As soon as you enter it, you will see a young donkey tied there that no one has ever ridden. Untie it and bring it here.

If anyone asks, 'What are you doing?' just say, 'The Lord needs it and will return it soon.'"

The two disciples left and found the colt standing in the street, tied outside the front door. As they were untying it, some bystanders demanded, "What are you doing, untying that colt?"

They said what Jesus had told them to say, and they were permitted to take it.

Then they brought the colt to Jesus and threw their garments over it, and he sat on it.

Many in the crowd spread their garments on the road ahead of him, and others spread leafy branches they had cut in the fields.

Jesus was in the center of the procession, and the people all around him were shouting,

"Praise God! Blessings on the one who comes in the name of the Lord!

Blessings on the coming Kingdom of our ancestor David!

Praise God in highest heaven!"

Devotional Thought

Jesus didn't sneak into Jerusalem—He commanded the streets. He entered with authority that couldn't be ignored. Even before He rode in, He gave His disciples specific instructions about the donkey. And just like that, the animal was released into their care because of who He was. This wasn't random; it was the weight of His name. When they said, "The Lord needs it," no one argued. **That's the kind of authority Jesus carries—no negotiation required.**

But notice the humility of His choice. Jesus didn't send for a warhorse or a chariot. That would be a Lamborghini these days. He chose a colt—a young donkey that had never been ridden. Something like a Honda Civic. Not flashy, not intimidating, not what you'd expect from a king. Yet this was prophecy fulfilled: *"Look, your King is coming to you. He is humble, riding on a donkey."* (Zechariah 9:9). Jesus was declaring: *"I am King—but not the kind you were planning for. My power doesn't come through force, but through sacrifice."*

As He rode, the people laid garments and branches on the road—an act of honor reserved for royalty. The whole scene looked like a parade, but it was more than celebration. It was declaration: *The true King has arrived.* The crowd shouted with boldness, praising Him as the one who brings God's Kingdom. And when the Pharisees wanted to shut it down, Jesus made it clear—even if the people stayed quiet, creation itself would erupt in praise.

This entry wasn't just a ride—it was a statement. Jesus wasn't hiding. He was walking (and riding) straight into His mission, straight into enemy territory, straight into the very city where He knew He would be betrayed and crucified. Bold, unshaken, fully in control. The King had arrived—and nothing could stop the sound of His glory.

Reflection Questions

1. **Where in my life am I avoiding bold steps that Jesus would walk right into?**

- Am I silent when I should be declaring His truth?
- Where do I need holy courage to stand up and step forward?

_____

_____

_____

_____

_____

_____

_____

2. **Would I have joined the crowd shouting His praises—or stood back like the Pharisees, uneasy about it all?**

- Do I hold back in worship because I fear what others think?
- What keeps me from praising Him openly and boldly?

_____

_____

_____

_____

_____

_____

_____

_____

112

3. **Do I honor Jesus as King—or just treat Him as convenient when I need help?**

- Am I letting Him command every part of my life—or only the areas I'm comfortable surrendering?
- Do I live as if He's Lord, or just as if He's useful?

_____

_____

_____

_____

_____

_____

_____

_____

_____

Prayer

Jesus,

Thank You for being the kind of King who doesn't hide or sneak in but walks with authority, humility, and purpose. Thank You for showing me that true power doesn't come from force but from obedience to the Father. Teach me to honor You as King over every part of my life. Let my praise be bold, loud, and unashamed—because You are worthy, and nothing can silence the truth of who You are.
Amen.

DAY 20

ONLY ONE WAY

Scripture Reading

John 14:1–7 (NLT)

"Don't let your hearts be troubled. Trust in God, and trust also in me. There is more than enough room in my Father's home. If this were not so, would I have told you that I am going to prepare a place for you? When everything is ready, I will come and get you, so that you will always be with me where I am.
And you know the way to where I am going."
"No, we don't know, Lord," Thomas said. "We have no idea where you are going, so how can we know the way?"
Jesus told him, "I am the way, the truth, and the life. No one can come to the Father except through me.
If you had really known me, you would know who my Father is. From now on, you do know him and have seen him!"

Devotional Thought

Jesus lays it out plain: "I am the way, the truth, and the life." No gray areas, no shortcuts, no "other ways" to sneak in. He said, "I'm the key—that's it. No spares. No backup combos."

What's wild is that Jesus is walking straight toward His crucifixion, but instead of panicking, He's giving His followers comfort. He tells them He's leaving—but not forever. He's going to set things up for them, and there's plenty of space. It's like He's saying: *"Come through. We got room."*

And when Thomas spoke up in doubt, Jesus didn't clap back or shame him. He gave truth. He reminded them that to know Him is to know the Father, and the way forward is through Him alone.

Jesus was calm under pressure. Compassionate yet firm. Focused on the mission and unshaken by fear or doubt. That's not just His posture—it's the example He left us.

Reflection Questions

1. **Where am I letting my heart be troubled instead of trusting that Jesus has already made a way?**

- How would my perspective change if I remembered He's not shaken by my panic or doubt?

_____

_____

_____

_____

_____

_____

_____

2. **Where am I holding back my real fears, doubts, and confusion?**

- Am I hiding what I feel—or can I trust that Jesus can handle my honesty?

_____

_____

_____

_____

_____

_____

_____

3. **Do I treat Jesus as *the* way—or just *one* way among many?**

- What other "ways" do I run to for comfort or truth?
- What needs to be surrendered so Jesus is my only option?

_____

_____

_____

_____

_____

_____

_____

_____

Prayer

Jesus,
Thank You for being the way, the truth, and the life. Thank You for not leaving me in fear or confusion but offering peace when my heart feels troubled. I don't want to treat You as just one option—I want to trust You as the only way. Help me bring my doubts and questions to You, knowing You can handle them. Prepare my heart as You prepare a place for me.
Amen.

DAY 21

THE FINAL WORD

Scripture Reading

Matthew 28:16–20 (NLT)

Then the eleven disciples left for Galilee, going to the mountain where Jesus had told them to go.
When they saw him, they worshiped him—but some of them doubted!
Jesus came and told his disciples, "I have been given all authority in heaven and on earth.
Therefore, go and make disciples of all the nations, baptizing them in the name of the Father and the Son and the Holy Spirit.
Teach these new disciples to obey all the commands I have given you. And be sure of this: I am with you always, even to the end of the age."

Devotional Thought

This is it—the closing act. Jesus had already done the impossible: He died and then got back up. And not just that—He spent time with the same crew who had mostly abandoned Him in His darkest hour. No shaming. No payback. Just grace, meals, and presence.

But when it was time to go, Jesus didn't fade out quietly. He stood on the full authority given to Him, declared it boldly, and passed that authority straight to His disciples. He didn't give them busywork—He gave them the *mission*. Global. Eternal. Life-changing.

He sent them to disciple, to teach, to baptize, and to spread His kingdom everywhere. And He didn't just drop the command and dip out. He sealed it with a promise: *"I am with you always."*

The one who defeated death, walked out of the grave, and proved He ain't no punk now calls His people to walk in that same boldness. His authority covers us. His presence goes with us. His mission defines us.

This isn't just the disciples' calling—it's ours. No shrinking back. No soft energy. Jesus ended His earthly ministry the same way He lived it: unshakable, fearless, loving, and in full authority.

Reflection Questions

1. **Do I live like Jesus truly has all authority—or do I let other powers (fear, culture, money, politics, opinions) outrank Him?**

- Where do I need to step out in confidence, remembering His authority covers me?

_____

_____

_____

_____

_____

_____

_____

2. **Who is Jesus leading me to disciple, mentor, or encourage—even if it feels inconvenient or uncomfortable?**

- Am I playing it safe with my faith or am I embracing the bold, worldwide vision Jesus gave His followers?

_____

_____

_____

_____

_____

_____

_____

3. **When do I forget that Jesus is always with me?**

- How would my daily life shift if I moved with constant awareness of His steady presence?

_____

_____

_____

_____

_____

_____

_____

_____

Prayer

Jesus,

Thank You for what You did on the cross—and for rising again for me. Thank You for trusting me with Your great commission. Help me to live it out in my everyday life with boldness, confidence, and love. You didn't leave us with soft energy but with authority and power. Let me walk in it and make the most of every opportunity to help others encounter You.

I want my life to declare to the world that You ain't no punk—and because You're with me, neither am I.
Amen.

Closing Note:
Jesus Ain't No Punk —
Neither Are We

From the wilderness to the cross, from dinner tables to temple courts, from calling the outcast to commissioning the church, we've walked through the bold and unapologetic life of Jesus. Over and over again, He proved that He ain't no punk.

- He stood toe-to-toe with temptation and came out stronger.

- He called out hypocrisy, corruption, and empty religion without backing down.

- He walked boldly into enemy territory, never sneaking, never hiding.

- He welcomed sinners, elevated the broken, and defended the rejected when no one else would.

- He healed the sick, raised the dead, and showed power that even demons had to respect.

- He set the record straight, told the truth even when it offended, and lived on mission with focus and fire.

- And finally—He laid down His life, picked it back up again, and passed His authority to us.

This devotional journey wasn't just about watching Jesus flex His authority and courage—it's about us realizing what that means for our own lives. If Jesus ain't no punk, and we're His followers, then neither are we.

That means:

- We don't shrink back when truth costs us something.

- We don't live small when Jesus calls us to go big.

- We don't let fear, culture, politics, money, or opinions outrank His authority.

- We don't keep silent when we're called to speak, and we don't just play "church" when we're called to be the Church.

Jesus left us His mission and His presence. The Great Commission wasn't the end—it was the beginning. The fire He carried is now the fire we carry. The authority He walked in is the same authority we live in.

So now the charge is simple: Live bold. Live unshaken. Live like Jesus is King. Live like Jesus ain't no punk—and neither are you.